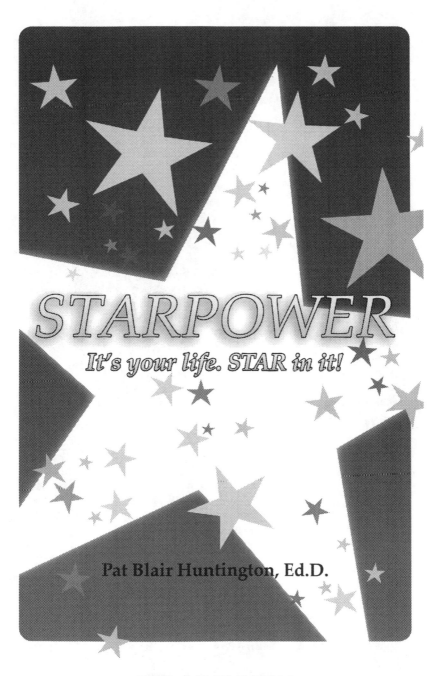

STARPOWER

It's your life. STAR in it!

Pat Blair Huntington, Ed.D.

ARCHWAY
PUBLISHING

Archway Publishing books may be ordered through booksellers or by contacting:

Archway Publishing
1663 Liberty Drive
Bloomington, IN 47403
www.archwaypublishing.com
1 (888) 242-5904

Because of the dynamic nature of the Internet, any web addresses or links contained in this book may have changed since publication and may no longer be valid. The views expressed in this work are solely those of the author and do not necessarily reflect the views of the publisher, and the publisher hereby disclaims any responsibility for them.

Any people depicted in stock imagery provided by Thinkstock are models, and such images are being used for illustrative purposes only. Certain stock imagery © Thinkstock.

STAR POWER is a copyrighted program developed by Pat Blair Huntington, Ed. D. and consultant Christine Cooper Oliphant, M.Ed.. Both have extensive experience with young adults in educational settings and are Licensed Professional Counselors.

Use of any material requires donation to the Star Power
501(c)(3) nonprofit for career development

Resources and referrals are based on information available at the time of publication. Students are encouraged to discuss any proposed purchase and/or recommendations with a qualified advisor.

Dr. Pat Blair Huntington
starpowerusa@yahoo.com
2449 Crosswind
Austin, Texas 78669

ISBN: 978-1-4808-4072-0 (sc)
ISBN: 978-1-4808-4073-7 (e)

Library of Congress Control Number: 2016921538

Print information available on the last page.

Archway Publishing rev. date: 1/5/2017

Thank YOU!

Christine Cooper, M.Ed., LPC, continues to be a collaborator on Star Power. Our work with thousands of teens in educational settings is an attempt to fill gaps in lifestyle and career education.

Contents

Introduction

Ready for a new destination or a more exciting future?

Life offers limitless opportunities beyond what is happening today.

Situations such as relationships, career options, living situations and health conditions may change. Some are beyond personal control.

Some days promise the best is yet to come and some the worse will never end. It helps to look back and remember that one year ago, this event or situation was not possible and one year from now, it may not be significant. Being accepted is blissful. Being rejected is endless pain.

STAR POWER reminds us that there is an unknown galaxy of opportunities with SHINE. SHINE provides a galaxy guide with directions for reaching a destination. The promises of something new can only happen with successes, failures, loves, losses and highs and lows during the journey.

It's your life, STAR in it.

Intro
It's Your Life. Star in It!

Star Power requires achievement, attitude, and aptitude. Too often, achievement is the primary concern of schools whereas future employers will often seek out the attitude and aptitude in an applicant. If achievement is slipping, approach it with a new attitude and apply an aptitude to tackle the approach. You may learn through reading, listening, or doing skills, so know how you learn best. Your control of the three A's (achievement, attitude, and aptitude) will help you achieve your dreams.

To begin your Star Power journey, begin with a selfie assessment. It reveals a starting point to the Star Power Certificate of Completion that certifies your personal commitment to success.

It's your life. Star Power is a limitless journey.

Selfie Assessment

Take the Star Power Selfie Assessment to reveal current self, social, and status indicators.

Self Identities reveal physical, intellectual, emotional, and spiritual attributes that reflect your image or branding.

Social Influences expose people, forces, and habits as motivators for life choices.

Status Incomes identify tangible rewards and intangible awards that impact lifestyle and success.

Check only for those statements that best describe you.

_____ 1   I eat healthy foods.

_____ 2   My work habits earn good results.

_____ 3   My behavior does not offend others.

_____ 4   I can tolerate those who disagree with me.

_____ 5   I live with good decision makers.

_____ 6   I obey rules at school or work.

_____ 7   I take care of my home and belongings.

_____ 8   I set goals for myself.

_____ 9   I feel respected in good ways.

_____ 10   I exercise daily or stay active.

_____ 11   I know about occupations that interest me.

_____ 12   I am happy more than sad.

_____ 13   I understand the history of other cultures.

_____ 14   I have one or more long-term friends.

_____ 15   I know how to say no to bad choices.

_____ 16   I don't act on impulse (ex. fights or chat rooms).

_____ 17 I earn my rewards.

_____ 18 Others ask for my opinion.

_____ 19 My health is good (vision, teeth, skin, etc.).

_____ 20 I use the library or Internet for assignments.

_____ 21 I learn from my mistakes.

_____ 22 I want to make the world a better place.

_____ 23 I have good people around me.

_____ 24 I accept the consequences of my poor choices.

_____ 25 I have good attendance standards.

_____ 26 I understand credit, debt, and contracts.

_____ 27 I commit to help others when I can.

_____ 28 I am able to sleep and get rest.

_____ 29 I find help when I need it (e.g., tutors).

_____ 30 I have safe outlets when depressed (e.g., journaling).

_____ 31 I work to improve my surroundings.

_____ 32 I work with people who are successful.

_____ 33 I know how state and federal laws impact me.

_____ 34 I have responsibilities at home that I complete.

_____ 35 I have a financial goal.

_____ 36 I am trustworthy with my assignments.

_____ 37 I like my appearance most of the time.

_____ 38 I excel in basics like math, spelling, and writing.

_____ 39 I avoid media, such as music, that depresses me.

_____ 40 I understand the dangers of gangs and cults.

_____ 41 I recognize positive people influences.

_____ 42 I avoid groups with unhealthy or unsafe goals.

_____ 43 I avoid any substance that steals my energy or happiness.

_____ 44 I have employable skills and habits.

_____ 45 I accept praise and give it.

Circle the numbers that you checked on the previous page.

The letter at the end of each row relates to an identity, influence, or income. Your strengths are the rows with the most circles.

1	10	19	28	37	P
2	11	20	29	38	I
3	12	21	30	39	E
4	13	22	31	40	S
5	14	23	32	41	PI
6	15	24	33	42	HI
8	17	26	35	44	TI
9	18	27	36	45	II

Using the Selfie Assessment, circle the Identity (P, I, E, S), Influence (PI, HI, FI), and Income (TI, II) that challenges your Star Power!

Self Identities
P Physical Identity
I Intellectual Identity
E Emotional Identity
S Spiritual Identity

Social Influences
PI People Influence
FI Force Influence
HI Habit Influence

Status Incomes
TI Tangible Income
II Intangible Income

The Selfie Assessment offers an opportunity to explore your star identities, influences, and incomes before you begin your journey. As you travel through Acts 1, 2, and 3, explore new possibilities for resolving problems, expand career options, and celebrate good life decisions.

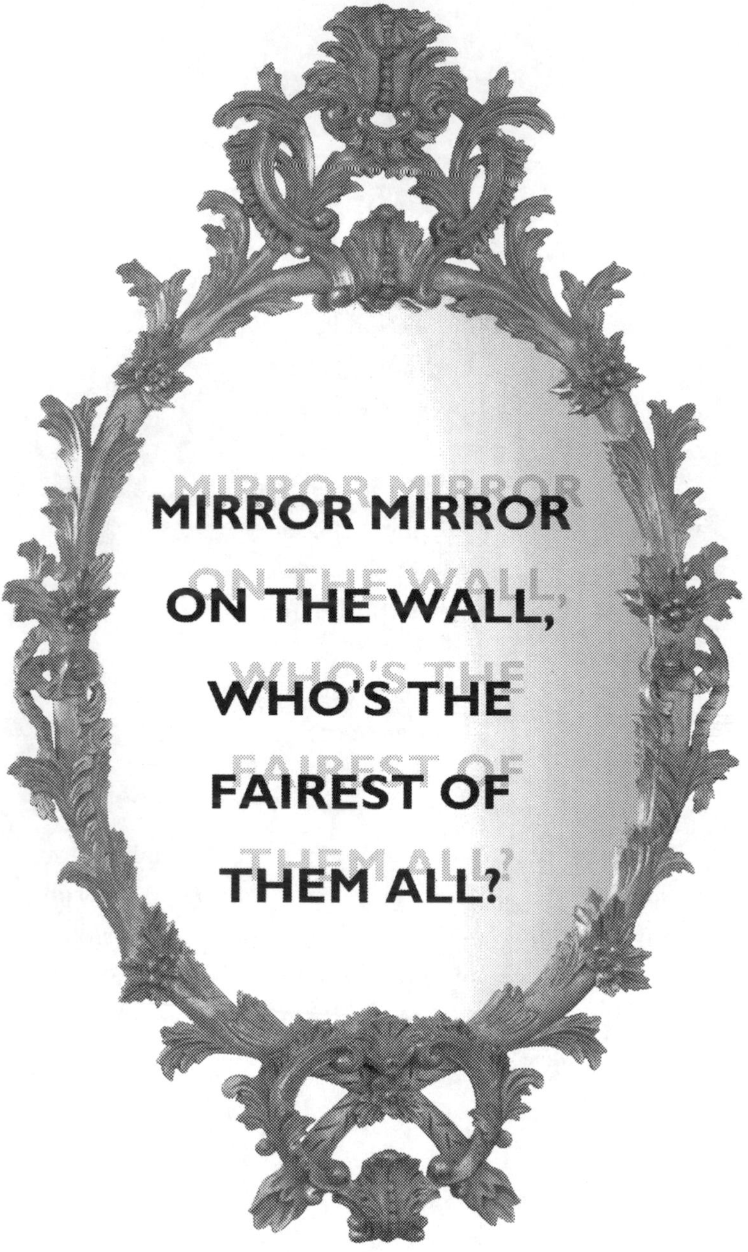

MIRROR MIRROR
ON THE WALL,
WHO'S THE
FAIREST OF
THEM ALL?

Act 1: My Self Identities

Stars are described by their brand qualities.

It's time to explore the **YOU** brand.

Identity is the sum total of your physical, intellectual, emotional, and spiritual self. Identities are your persona or how the world perceives you. As you review your characteristics, consider how they interact with one another. For instance, your identity may be influenced by friends and your income. Begin with your identities to build your brand recognition

Physical identity relates to your appearance and health.
Intellectual identity reveals your skills, talents, and academic intelligence.
Emotional identity explores the health of your moods and emotions.
Spirituality identity unlocks your value and belief system.

Candace is going to a holiday dance in three weeks. Her favorite dress no longer fits. She can't afford to join a club or diet plan. Her doctor had suggested she change her diet after a recent blood test indicated her cholesterol was too high. Family members have suffered from heart issues and diabetes, so she realizes there could be a genetic problem. Those diseases can alter her life activities.

She browses the Internet and checks food labels to find foods that are low in carbohydrates and sugars. Potatoes, breads, refried beans, potatoes, and rice are traded for colored vegetables. Ice cream and cookies are traded for berries and a can of whipped cream. She now eats butter, not chemicals. Snacks include fresh fruits and nuts. Portion control is also a new concern. She double-checks servings and calories. The cookie package actually has three, two hundred-calorie servings, not just one serving.

Cutting carbs and sugars are an easy solution. The dress fits, but it takes three weeks. Best of all, her energy and confidence have returned. A new blood test showed improvement. Her new diet is no longer a way for weight loss; it is a way of life.

Serving Size: It's usually less than people eat. When comparing foods, make sure the serving sizes are the same.

Fat: The total amount of fat in one serving.

Cholesterol: Eat less than 300 mg per day.

Sodium: (Salt) Eat less than 2400 mg per day.

Carbohydrates: Energy. Good source of fiber. Eat 20-35 g per day

Protein: Helps build muscle. Found in meat, nuts, eggs, fish and dry beans.

Calories: Measures the energy used.

% Daily Value: Recommended amount of nutrients per serving. Don't eat more than 100% of each nutrient per day.

Vitamins & Minerals: The recommended amount of vitamins and minerals found in the food. Reach 100% of each per day.

Recommended Amounts: Per nutrient. It depends on your age, gender and how active you are.

Self Identity: Physical

A first impression is hard to change.

Successful people tend to dress to create a good impression.

An impression involves appearance, including the condition of skin, teeth, hair, and clothing.

Speech patterns, accents, and grammar are part of your brand.

Weight is important, especially if it impacts your energy level, cholesterol, and general health. Genetics and family health history may be important for future medical concerns.

Typically, a change of lifestyle is necessary if an appearance change is desired. This may include a change in diet, sleep patterns, hygiene routines, and activities. Change requires commitment and that takes time. Old routines are hard to break.

Make a
good first
impression

Physical Identity

Which physical features do you consider your best? There is no perfect look, but there are good first impressions. Grade the impression you feel you make on others.

D (Poor) **C** (Fair) **B** (Good) **A** (Great) (Check ✓)

	D	C	B	A
Appropriate dress	—	—	—	—
Posture	—	—	—	—
Hygiene/cleanliness	—	—	—	—
Weight	—	—	—	—
Speech patterns	—	—	—	—
Hearing	—	—	—	—
Vision/eyesight	—	—	—	—
Style/dress	—	—	—	—
General health	—	—	—	—
Strength	—	—	—	—
Focus	—	—	—	—
Endurance	—	—	—	—

Star Resources

After reviewing your Physical Identity, check out the following resources and add your own:

Health

- ☐ Call dental schools and medical schools for low or no cost services. Be persistent.
- ☐ Talk to a local pharmacist about reading glasses or general medical advice.
- ☐ Get regular check ups.

Grooming

- ☐ Read online reviews of skin products.

Speech, Vision, Hearing

- ☐ Talk to your school counselor for help, call local colleges and talk to department heads for help and guidance as some offer free services. Ask for help. Get annual dental exam.

Physical Fitness

- ☐ Read fitness books.
- ☐ Visit health or physical fitness coaches at school.
- ☐ Talk to school nurse about nutrition. Reduce calories, carbs and sugars.
- ☐ Get physical.
- ☐ Hang out with people who promote healthy habits.
- ☐ Join a fitness club.
- ☐ Exercise daily.
- ☐ Become a dog walker.

Dress

- ☐ Visit resale shops when money is tight.
- ☐ Dress for success.

Self Identity: Intellectual

Cary hates school. Another day of feeling dumb. Another week of being grounded for bad grades. Another round of standardized testing with meaningless percentages. A local career fair expands Cary's knowledge about future career possibilities. He learns employers look at aptitude and attitude!

Good attendance and trade skills are not recognized on achievement tests. Cary's school only offers the ASVAB military aptitude test and career interest tests.

Cary finds an online aptitude test at www.edits.net that is low cost. He takes the test and matches his aptitude with engineering careers. He uses the Occupational Outlook Handbook (www.bls.gov.ooh) to research other career possibilities.

Cary is excited to know all of his potential!

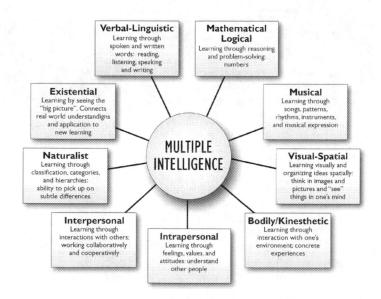

Self Identity: Intellectual

Your intellectual identity may be related to school success. However, there are intelligences that go beyond school subjects. Aptitude tests will help you discover abilities that could help you succeed in a career.

Schools give achievement and academic tests. The aptitude test may be a true predictor of your career success. For example, a surgeon requires fine motor dexterity to perform surgery. Aptitude tests explore your fine motor dexterity and other skills. Interning in a trade such as plumbing, computer drafting, and auto repair can become profitable careers or worthy training for other employment. With an understanding of your skills, you can focus on the training you need to improve your career strengths.

Ask your counselor to help you find an aptitude test to discover your abilities. *Beware of any online test that obligates you to a school or financial costs.* Use the tests to learn about yourself, and explore the results with your counselor. Read about careers in the Occupational Outlook Handbook (www.bls.gov/ooh).

Television and media glamorize work in professions. An actor or musician's life may look great but may require living poor or having two jobs for several years. . Before investing in trade school or college, check out the lifestyle, income, and job opportunities of what they offer. Verify that the debt is worth the investment. Contact companies and know the requirements and benefits. Teen years are preparation for life.

http://www.bls.gov/ooh
Occupational outlook handbook
— free on this site

Intellectual Identity

Check (✓) career fields that interest you.

D (No) **C** (Maybe) **B** (Like) **A** (Prefer)

	D	C	B	A
Architecture, Engineering				
Arts and Design				
Building and Grounds Cleaning				
Business and Financial				
Community and Social Service				
Computer and Information Technology				
Construction and Extraction				
Education, Training, and Library				
Entertainment and Sports				
Farming, Fishing, and Forestry				
Food Preparation and Serving				
Healthcare				
Installation, Maintenance, and Repair				
Legal				
Life, Physical, and Social Science				
Management				
Math				
Media and Communication				
Military				
Office and Administrative Support				
Personal Care and Service				
Production				
Protective Service				
Sales				
Transportation and Material Moving				

Star Resources

Aptitude tests

- ☐ Talk to a counselor about career or tests. Go to Edits web site, call them
- ☐ Visit websites that provide current employment information.
  Go to visit the resource website:
  http://www.bls.gov/ooh/

School search

- ☐ Match your aptitude skills with job skills. Visit websites of colleges, career schools, internships and apprentice programs. Compare costs of employment after completion of coursework. Would cost be a reasonable payback for income?

Employer search

- ☐ Compare costs of training with the salary you will receive. If the cost exceeds what you can pay back within one or two years, check out community colleges or on the job training opportunities. Avoid long term debt.

Part time opps

- ☐ Join clubs, get a part time job and volunteer to add experiences to college and job resumes.

Breakups are the worst. Caroline's breakup seems to be the end of everything. She can't study. Friends no longer include her in outings because they prefer hanging with her ex, who throws parties with his new girlfriend. Leaving a class and seeing the old group makes her anxious. She feels like she lives in a dark hole and is depressed. Her mother tells her to move on. But it is not her mother's life. It's Caroline's life! Even counselors suggest that school success is more important than feelings. She is facing the holidays and her birthday without somebody special again!

An article in a magazine reminds her that only a year ago she did not have this relationship. She realizes that she can meet new people. She tries a new daily schedule.

- ☆ Sad Time (only five minutes of telling a friend, crying)
- ☆ Study Time
- ☆ Opportunity Time (find a new hobby, job, or interest)
- ☆ Network Circle (connect with a new group)
- ☆ Charity or Care Group (make a difference)

Recovering from a breakup, getting fired from a job, or getting dropped from a team requires energy and determination to move on. It takes living one day at a time and knowing that promising times are ahead.  Caroline decides to change the L, or loser attitude, to LL, "lesson learned," and to take the next relationship a little slower.

Self Identity: Emotional

Moods and feelings may be described as healthy or unhealthy.

How do your actions reflect your emotional identity? Do you have an infantile "I want it now," demanding "Do it my way," or a stable "let's work together" emotional identity? How would others describe you? Healthy emotions suggest a good frame of mind and the ability to move forward and be proud of your actions. Unhealthy emotions, such as too much sharing on the Internet or creating drama with suggestive pictures, will only decrease your self-esteem.

Emotional health can be destroyed by the loss of a friend or family member, being rejected by others, or failing to reach a goal. These losses may impact your heart (feelings) or brain (decision making). only But life can get back on track. Few people have the same friends at three, thirteen, thirty-three, and fifty-three. And few people have the same goals at thirteen that they have at thirty-three.

During the next ten years, life will offer many possibilities. Accept that you may change locations, jobs, schools, and friendships. Build your emotional identity brand with friends, mentors, and career opportunities. Rarely does an intense physical relationship survive the teen years. It's your life. Explore safe, healthy possibilities.

Emotional identity warning signs may be a desire to hurt yourself or others, the need to consume alcohol or pills to feel okay, or continuing to remain upset. Addiction to the Internet is serious if it impacts your social or school success. Who is your mentor for times of stress or emotional problems?

Emotional Identity

Rate your behavior in these situations.

D (Poor Performance) C (Fair) B (Good) A (Great) (Check ✓)

	D	C	B	A
Class/work overload	__	__	__	__
Breakup/fight with friend	__	__	__	__
Discussion with parent or teacher	__	__	__	__
Not being invited to a party	__	__	__	__
Losing a contest/failing a test	__	__	__	__
Finishing long assignments	__	__	__	__
Starting assignments on time	__	__	__	__
Reactions to text, e-mails, Facebook	__	__	__	__
Driving a car in bad traffic	__	__	__	__
Being harassed or bullied	__	__	__	__
Being asked to break a rule	__	__	__	__
Handling weight problems	__	__	__	__
Decisions involving love or desires	__	__	__	__
Shopping to feel better	__	__	__	__
Add your own:	__	__	__	__
_____	__	__	__	__
_____	__	__	__	__
_____	__	__	__	__

Star Resources

Abusers

☐ Ask a counselor about an abuse hotline for friend being abused by family member.

www.teenshealth.org/teen/your_mind/best_self/choose-mood.html

Emotional IQ-what is it?

www.emotionalcompetency.com/personality traits.htm

Breakups

☐ Move on with new groups and a new schedule. DRAMA MAY JUST POSTPONE ENDING. Take few minutes every morning to be sad. Then, focus on the positive and remember times that problem did not exist. Look to the future for a time when problem will be just a memory. See a counselor if necessary. Use friends but don't abuse friends with problems.

Media

☐ Use Facebook or social media only for positive talk and pictures.

Check out app Rx: Breakup

☐ Relationships, jobs etc. Website for breakups

Self Identity: Spiritual

John's parents are churchgoers. His friends attend a nondenominational gathering at a local restaurant that meets on Tuesday nights. John tells his parents he wants to trade Sunday morning church for the Tuesday night meeting.

John explains that the group does charity work and talks about spirituality, but not a specific religion. He will continue with his Sunday night youth group at the church. His parents are upset but agree to the change. Understanding the relationship of spirituality and religion becomes a new discussion at home.

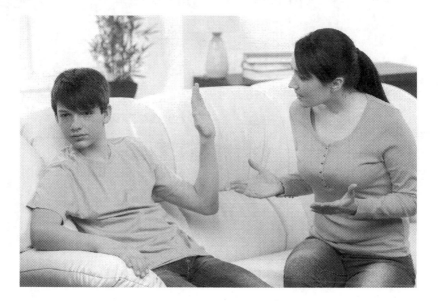

Self Identity: Spiritual

Spirituality takes on a different meaning with various cultures, religions, or even political organizations. Spirituality revolves around your beliefs and values. Spirituality considers the importance you put on life and relationships not only for yourself but also for others. The Golden Rule, "Do unto others as you would have others do to you," is an example.

Religion is the foundation of many civilizations. Cultural films, books, and family stories involve religious themes. Expanding your knowledge about religion helps you understand some political wars and social conflicts. The Bible is one resource.

Religion may involve specific beliefs in relation to God or deities whereas spirituality embraces values and beliefs. How you care for your body and treat others reveals your values. How you vote and involve yourself in society often depends on your beliefs.

Your spiritual self may impact your identities, influences, and income. Your life may include spirituality with or without ties to any formalized religion. Religion may be the source or pillar for spirituality. Consider how your values and beliefs impact your home life, schoolwork, and social network. Do you belong to any group that supports spirituality, such as mission trips or charity events?

Spiritual Identity

Explore your Spiritual Identity

D (No Impact) **C** (Maybe) **B** (Some Impact)
A (Great Impact) Check✓

	D	C	B	A
Religious views	__	__	__	__
Church membership	__	__	__	__
Cultural (family history)	__	__	__	__
Political impact	__	__	__	__
Charity involvement	__	__	__	__
Friendships	__	__	__	__
Social clubs	__	__	__	__
Ethics (morals)	__	__	__	__
Add your own	__	__	__	__
	__	__	__	__
	__	__	__	__
	__	__	__	__

Star Resources

News and religion

❑ Search the news and find some impact that spirituality and religion has on life today

Founding fathers

❑ How do the beliefs and values in the US Constitution and Bill of Rights differ from other countries?

❑ How have these beliefs and values contributed to the wealth and health of the country?

Religion/spirituality

❑ How do religion, spirituality and politics conflict or agree with each other?

Voting

❑ How do spirituality and good citizenship impact each other?

Describe your brand:

Write an ad for yourself advertising for a career or club position.

Appearance:

Intellect (achievement, aptitude):

Emotion (adult, child, infant):

Spiritual (values, beliefs):

How is your brand received in different settings?

Home:

School:

Club:

Crowds:

Employment:

Act 2: My Social Influences

Influences Impact Today and Tomorrow

Consider how influences impact your network of friends, appearance, success, and behaviors.

Social influences include

People influences
People (real or fictional) with direct or indirect persuasion

Force influences
Rules, laws, guidelines, and social manners

Habit influences
Activities that result in success or failure

David has a big decision.

The science club will be going to an overnight school conference on Saturday. At the same time there is a concert that his friends will attend.

The party after the concert will be unchaperoned, and David's parents would not approve. He could face losing car privileges.

The science club event will help his grade average. However, the concert will be time with the most popular people in school.

This is David's chance to spend time with a new girl who wants him to party. His friend is giving him a hard time about not going to the party.

Social Influences: People

People can be powerful influences in your making life choices.

People influences are direct when they impact decisions like earning grades, making friends, or planning a future.

People influences are indirect when you listen to their suggestions about dress or less important decisions.

Parents, school mentors, friends, acquaintances, celebrities, and sometimes real or fictional media characters become indirect and direct influences. Have you ever noticed how a friend mimics the dress or character of a celebrity?

Often you are judged by the associations and influences in your life. Consider the length and strength the influence will have on your adult life. Will that influence remain with you in good and bad times? It's your life. Choose wisely.

Show me your friends and I will show you your future.

People Influences

Who impacts your life activities
and decisions? Check ✓

D (Direct Influence) **I** (Indirect Influence, or Some or None)

	D	I
Male family member	—	—
Female family member	—	—
Academic teacher	—	—
Counselor or school administrator	—	—
Coach	—	—
Male friend	—	—
Female friend	—	—
Community or religious leader	—	—
Media stars and celebrities	—	—
Internet friends	—	—
Heroes in news	—	—
Business leader	—	—
Significant person	—	—
Fictional character	—	—
Add your own:	—	—
_____	—	—
_____	—	—
_____	—	—

Star Resources

Heros
find a community, national international hero for class paper.

Villains
–review the lives of community, national and international bad guys for psychology paper.

Politicians
–join a party and learn the politics of my city, state, and nation so you can be a learned voter. Check facts.

Financial
find out about bank accounts and credit cards. Also talk to teachers about how to avoid debt.

Circle of Friends
Make a list for future party.

Counselors
–financial aid info and references.

Social Influences: Forces

Attendance at school for Katie is getting hard. With a night job, getting to school on time is a real problem.

After school detention, Katie was speeding to work and got a ticket. The police officer then found an open beer can in the car. Her mother grounded her from social events. She can't win for the rules. Katie needs an ally.

Her counselor suggests that she evaluate her schedule and invites her mother in for a conference. Katie negotiates for before-school detention until her job hours can be changed.

Social Influences: Forces

Forces are social influences when they establish boundaries. Forces, such as school policies and governmental laws, protect you and others from chaos by establishing structure.

It is how you respond to these forces that impacts your present and future star power. For instance, breaking a school rule may result in detention but breaking a governmental rule like drinking while driving or stealing could impact your life for a long time. Driving while texting that results in a death could be a lifelong punishment for an unintentional lapse in judgment.

Forces provide society with structure. Manners allow females to enter the room first or dictate which fork to use during dinner. Rules that seem silly may provide a structure that makes sense. For instance, making a phone call late in the night not only breaks courtesy rules but also alarms a family that may think there is an emergency.

Rules control classroom discussion, such as raising your hand to speak. Rules and manners make life choices easy. It's your life. **May the good forces be with you.**

Proceed with caution.

Force Influences

What forces guide you? Check✓

N (Never) **D** (Direct, or Often) **I** (Indirect, or Sometimes)

	N	D	I
School rules and guidelines	__	__	__
Home rules	__	__	__
Club rules	__	__	__
Employment or boss	__	__	__
City or state laws	__	__	__
International laws and passports	__	__	__
Religious or spiritual guidelines	__	__	__
Internet, media	__	__	__
Social demands	__	__	__
Good manners	__	__	__
Add your own	__	__	__
_____	__	__	__
_____	__	__	__
_____	__	__	__

Star Resources

☐ **Teenagers and the law:**
Check out laws related to age.

☐ **How old he needs to be:**
To open a bank account, join a political party, get a tattoo, see a doctor alone, consent to medical treatment, learn to drive, get a part-time job or be left at home alone.

☐ **Debt:**
Talk to banker re credit ratings

☐ **Insurance:**
What does insurance cover and what does it not cover

☐ **Consensual relationships:**
Check out laws about how I imply *YES*

Social Influences: Habits

Doctors give Sara medicine for anxiety, but it causes depression. Then she takes night medication for sleep. She wants a better way, such as meditation, instead of medication. To manage anxiety, some of Sara's friends drink and stop at one, but one drink is never enough for Sara.

Family and friends have addictions, i.e., full body tattoos, pills, booze, even "free money" from big allowances. Everything is done in excess. Debt and stress seem to be an endless cycle without any self-control.

Sara changes to a doctor and a counselor who are not pill-happy but care about her physically. She replaces happy hours with time at the gym. Her old friends shun her, but she finds a social club to join through her school. Drama is down, but her spirits are up.

Sara wants a different life. Bad habits impact relationships, employment, debt, and stress. She wants a good life.

Social Influences: Habits

Habits impact daily life. They may dictate your activity schedule, food choices, social involvement, or work routine.

Habits require self-discipline to maintain or to change. Negative habits, such as addictions (food, alcohol, drugs), put your physical, intellectual, emotional, and spiritual self at risk. They also impact your income.

Negative habits can ruin relationships and destroy goals.

Habits that add to your star power help regulate use of time, encourage you to complete tasks, and build positive relationships. It's your life. "Your actions become your habits, your habits become your values and your values become your destiny." (Mahatma Gandhi)

Behavior predicts behavior.

Habit Influences

Consider the habits that have positive
impact on your Star Power. (Check ✓)

	Yes	No
Hygiene or health issues	___	___
Grades or academic standing	___	___
Good manners	___	___
Being on time	___	___
Completing tasks	___	___
Diet or physical fitness	___	___
Internet, media	___	___
Spending habits	___	___
Housekeeping	___	___
Organization of work and clothes	___	___
Add your own	___	___
_____	___	___
_____	___	___
_____	___	___

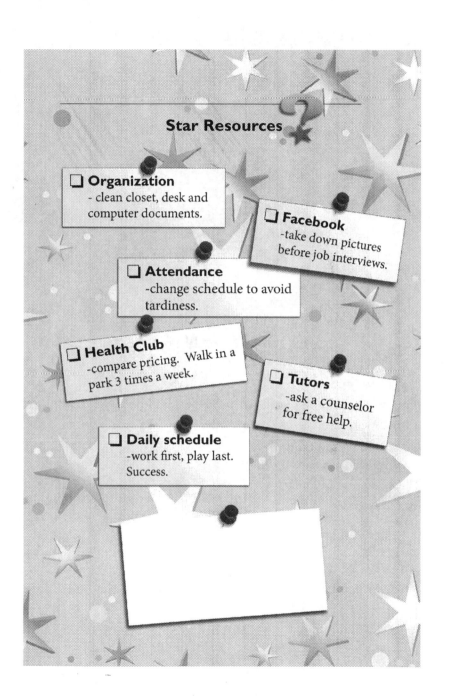

Star Resources

Organization
- clean closet, desk and computer documents.

Facebook
-take down pictures before job interviews.

Attendance
-change schedule to avoid tardiness.

Health Club
-compare pricing. Walk in a park 3 times a week.

Tutors
-ask a counselor for free help.

Daily schedule
-work first, play last. Success.

Act 3: My Status Income

**Status income can either be tangible
(money) or intangible (respect).**

Tangible Income
is negotiable, like cash, and can be exchanged for necessities or gifts.
Tangible income needs to exceed debt for successful living.

Intangible Income
may be applause, a thank you, or recognition for doing a good deed
or job.

Status Income: Tangible

Julio's first paycheck was a real shocker. He thought he would receive $2,500, but his check was about $2,000. Nobody had ever fully explained payroll deductions and the difference between gross income ($2,500) and net income ($2,000).

His expense on a new credit card exceeded his net earnings. His $2,200 credit card bill will take two years to pay off if he pays the minimum payment each month, and that is all he can afford. It will add at least $500 in interest. A new job and Julio already is in debt.

Julio learns that a friend moved into an expensive apartment after graduation with a one-year lease. He lost his job but must still pay for the lease, so now he works two jobs just to support his apartment. He needs a roommate.

Julio's job is the result of his good school attendance and character references. It is his first job, and he needs to save for a college course to keep the position.

Julio decides that unless he learns about finance and budgeting, he may never be able to live without debt. He has to change his lifestyle and reduce the $300 he now spends on Internet, cable, and phone.

Status Income: Tangible

Academic transcripts are your tangible income (paycheck) from your school.

A paycheck is a tangible income from employment. Other types of tangible income include travel allowances and scholarships. Tangible income is a reward that provides you a better life or opportunities as an independent adult.

Tangible income increases with the willingness to take a job others refuse or to learn new skills that have worth to a company or organization. Employment may require you to take a training position, work in a warehouse, or start as a mail clerk. Employers need to know you before they invest valuable training time in your future.

Education and skills are all around you. Check with your local hardware store for classes on home repair that can help you find part-time work. Find out what skill classes in school make you employable. A future engineer may benefit from a CAD (computer-aided design) class. A future CPA (certified public accountant) needs accounting or business math. Use the Occupational Outlook Handbook to learn about skills you need. It's your life. Learning is your lifetime friend.

Prosperity/poverty is a way of living and thinking and not just a lack of money or things.
—Eric Butterworth

Tangible Income

How would you rate your tangible income? Check ✓

NS (Not Satisfied) **S** (Satisfied)

	NS	S
Grades, academic standing	___	___
Regular employment	___	___
Savings or controlling spending	___	___
Part-time employment	___	___
Use of coupons, discounts	___	___
Sale of unused items	___	___
Research scholarships or career	___	___
School opportunities	___	___
Understanding of credit cards, contracts	___	___
Understanding of interest on debt	___	___
Ability to keep a job	___	___
Willingness to learn skill for a job	___	___
Current job skills	___	___
Understanding aptitude skills	___	___
Add your own	___	___
_____	___	___
_____	___	___
_____	___	___

Star Resources

☐ **Income**
– study pay stubs to learn about gross and net pay.

☐ **Contracts**
- learn about lease, phone and credit card contracts.

☐ **Grades**
- find what grades and courses help with internships and scholarships.

☐ **Budget**
- save money with coupons, live on a budget, get extra job for debt.

☐ **Safety**
- ask employer about safety regulations and guidelines (lifting, chemicals).

☐ **Buy it or NOT?**
- Do I really need this? Why do I really want it? Will I use it? Wear it?
http://www.themint.org/teens/buy-it-or-not.html

☐ www.daveramsey.com
Course for learning how to budget.

Status Income: Intangible

Working as a volunteer at the hospital paid off for Kara in getting her first job. Although the time for volunteerism did not provide income, the recommendation for her work proved to help her with a college scholarship and a part-time job at the college hospital.

Status Income: Intangible

Honor and respect seem like old-fashioned perks for hard work. It is also a odd way to get paid but may award you in a different and even more lasting payoff. Your self-esteem opens doors to healthy friendships and career possibilities.

Another way to make a good impression is through helping others. Working with others on a community project or as a tutor allows you to build character references.

Employers may look at good attendance and attitude, which mean more than high grades. Your willingness and ability to show up on time is critical in some jobs. How would you feel if you were a shift worker and could not leave until your replacement clocked in to work?

It's your life. Awards may become your greatest rewards.

Intangible Income

Evaluate your current intangible income. Check✓

NS (Not Satisfied) **S** (Satisfied)

	NS	S
Attendance awards	__	__
Leadership roles	__	__
Charity or community involvement	__	__
Compliments for manners, habits	__	__
Self-discipline in bad situations	__	__
Acknowledgment by those you respect	__	__
Acceptance from others	__	__
Honesty	__	__
Loyalty	__	__
Responsibility with pets, children	__	__
Promotions at work or school	__	__
Add your own	__	__
_____	__	__
_____	__	__
_____	__	__
_____	__	__
_____	__	__

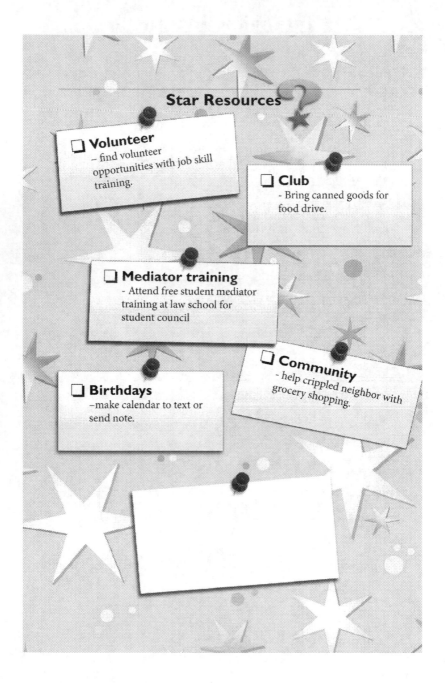

Star Resources

❑ Volunteer
– find volunteer opportunities with job skill training.

❑ Club
- Bring canned goods for food drive.

❑ Mediator training
- Attend free student mediator training at law school for student council

❑ Community
- help crippled neighbor with grocery shopping.

❑ Birthdays
–make calendar to text or send note.

Acts I, II and III introduced you to three elements of Star Power:

Your Personal Identity

(physical, intellectual, emotional and spiritual)

Your Social Influences

(people, forces, habits)

Your Status Income

(tangible rewards and intangible awards)

Assess yourself and then SHINE in Act IV

Script Challenge

Consider how STAR POWER identity, influences and income impact your Star power in different settings:

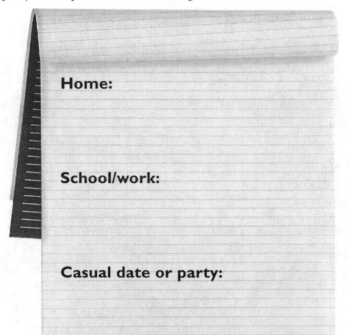

Home:

School/work:

Casual date or party:

Formal event:

Write a movie title that would describe your life today.
Describe your role and the main characters.

Act 4: My Status Destination: SHINE

SHINE is your Star Power destination roadmap.

Enhance your self-identity, social influences, and status income with SHINE.

SHINE is an acronym that provides a guide for life decisions.

S Set point (the goal you want to reach)

H Heroes (people who take risks for you or invest in you)

I Investment (time and resources you need to succeed)

N Negatives (setbacks or speed bumps that may occur)

E "Enerobics" (Star Power term that combines energy and action necessary to succeed. Without enerobic efforts, you make little progress because all goals require energy and action.)

Example of SHINE

S Set point: pass algebra

H Heroes: tutor, advisor, job coach

I Investment: time for study, resources to pay tutor

N Negatives: less social time, summer school

E Enerobics: energy from healthy lifestyle and action that keeps you on schedule.

SHINE begins with a Set Point

Describe a set point for your self identities, social influences, and status incomes.

Set Points

My Self Identities
Physical_____

_____

Intellectual_____

_____

Emotional_____

_____

Spiritual_____

_____

My Social Influences
People_____

_____

Forces_____

_____

Habits_____

_____

My Status Income
Tangible_____

_____

Intangible_____

_____

SHINE needs Heroes

Describe a Hero for your self identities, social influences, and status incomes.

Heros

My Self Identities
Physical_____

_____

Intellectual_____

_____

Emotional_____

_____

Spiritual_____

_____

My Social Influences
People_____

_____

Forces_____

_____

Habits_____

_____

My Status Income
Tangible_____

_____

Intangible_____

_____

SHINE requires Investment

Describe investments (time and resources) for achieving your self identities, social influences, and status incomes.

Investments

My Self Identities
Physical_____

_____

Intellectual_____

_____

Emotional_____

_____

Spiritual_____

_____

My Social Influences
People_____

_____

Forces_____

_____

Habits_____

_____

My Status Income
Tangible_____

_____

Intangible_____

_____

SHINE accepts Negatives

Describe negatives that could impact goals for your self identities, social influences, and status incomes.

Negatives

My Self Identities
Physical_____

_____

Intellectual_____

_____

Emotional_____

_____

Spiritual_____

_____

My Social Influences
People_____

_____

Forces_____

_____

Habits_____

_____

My Status Income
Tangible_____

_____

Intangible_____

_____

SHINE excels with Enerobics

Describe an enerobic activity for your self identities, social influences, and status incomes.

Enerobics

My Self Identities
Physical_____

_____

Intellectual_____

_____

Emotional_____

_____

Spiritual_____

_____

My Social Influences
People_____

_____

Forces_____

_____

Habits_____

_____

My Status Income
Tangible_____

_____

Intangible_____

_____

After a few goals are reached with SHINE, the process will become part of your decision-making process.

Don't give up, especially in difficult situations. Passing one test, dieting one week, or making one friend rarely makes you SHINE. The solution may take as long or longer than it took to create the problem. Winning a race or contest may take several tries. Give yourself credit for each step you accomplish. YOU have Star Power. All you need is SHINE.

It's YOUR time to SHINE!

Congratulations!

Your future star-power years may require independent living, employment, change of school, new friends, and **STAR POWER** aims to provide tools for safe, healthy, debt-free possibilities. You are more than a grade in school, a member of a class, or a friend. You are a STAR in the making.

STAR POWER uses SHINE as a goal-setting tool after interactive sessions about relationships. self-identity, social influences, and status-income relationships are reviewed as a reminder of their impact on today's and future goals.

STAR POWER was developed for you after years of working with teens struggling to make good choices about relationships, education, and careers. This journal encourages you to meet with mentors, counselors, parents, physicians, teachers, and websites to unleash your potential.

STAR POWER offers a website for you to blog or ask questions related to your experiences. The website is sponsored by donations to STAR POWER Inc., a 501(c)(3) charity, and is free for you to visit at www.starpowerusa.com.

STAR POWER may be used in counseling, educational, and club settings by sending an e-mail to Dr. Pat Huntington at starpowerusa@yahoo.com. All copyrighted materials must have permission for duplication or use in any commercial activity.

Display your certificate with pride. It requires focus and commitment to be a **STAR POWER** graduate.

Shine on!

Certification
Of
Completion

This Certifies That

_____

has successfully completed the training program
for

Star Power

Enhancing Self, Social
and Status Relationships

_____   _____
Date   Signed

SHINE GUIDE

Are you ready for independent living?

D (Not Ready) C (Soon) B (Need Help) A (Ready) Check✓

	D	C	B	A
Living alone	__	__	__	__
Finding and keeping a job	__	__	__	__
Food preparation and housekeeping	__	__	__	__
Transportation	__	__	__	__
Handling money	__	__	__	__
Ability to handle emergencies	__	__	__	__
Personal safety	__	__	__	__
Handing problems	__	__	__	__
Finding and supporting living space	__	__	__	__
Communicating with professionals	__	__	__	__
Selecting responsible roommates	__	__	__	__

Are you ready for a relationship?

D (No) **C** (Rarely) **B** (Often) **A** (Yes) Check✓

	D	C	B	A
Do you have one good friend or more?	__	__	__	__
Do you balance friendships with obligations?	__	__	__	__
Do you have personal goals ?	__	__	__	__
Do you like yourself?	__	__	__	__
Do your parents/guardians approve of your dating?	__	__	__	__
Do you group date?	__	__	__	__
Do you trust yourself to set limits (texting, curfew)?	__	__	__	__
Do you consider yourself a jealous person?	__	__	__	__
Do you consider a trusting friendship the first step?	__	__	__	__
Do you accept that future commitments may require separation from this person?	__	__	__	__
Do you continue other relationships and activities?	__	__	__	__
Is a relationship more about status than the person?	__	__	__	__

Are you ready for employment?

D (No) **C** (Rarely) **B** (Often) **A** (Yes) Check ✓

	D	C	B	A
Can you work each week?	__	__	__	__
Can you give up texting and other habits during work time?	__	__	__	__
Can you do simple math, such as 45+78, 128-49, 15% of 245, 15/90?	__	__	__	__
Can you define and spell words that sound Alike, such as *know* and *no*?	__	__	__	__
Can you make change for $20, $50, $100?	__	__	__	__
Can you read and complete an employment application?	__	__	__	__
Can you focus on a task until you learn it?	__	__	__	__
Can you accept a boss telling you what to do?	__	__	__	__
Can you accept that you may hear no if you work in sales?	__	__	__	__
Can you accept that customers are not always happy but you must be?	__	__	__	__
Can you write or print for others to read?	__	__	__	__
Can you dress appropriately for your job?	__	__	__	__

SHINE
physical, intellectual, emotional and spiritual identities

Consider feeling healthier, achieving more, controlling moods, and appreciating your values.

Setpoint

Heroes

Investment

Negatives

Enerobics

SHINE
people, forces and habit influences

Consider how your interactions with people, forces such as the legal system and improving habits will increase your STAR POWER.

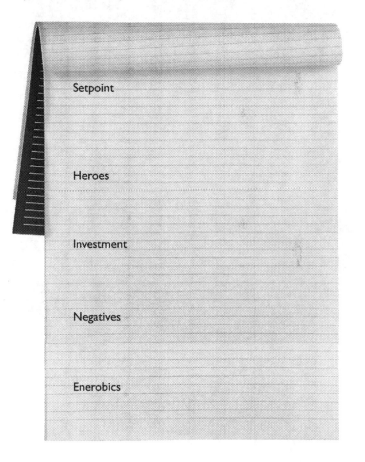

Setpoint

Heroes

Investment

Negatives

Enerobics

SHINE
tangible and intangible incomes

Consider your future education and career opportunities. Include time in your life for intangible incomes.

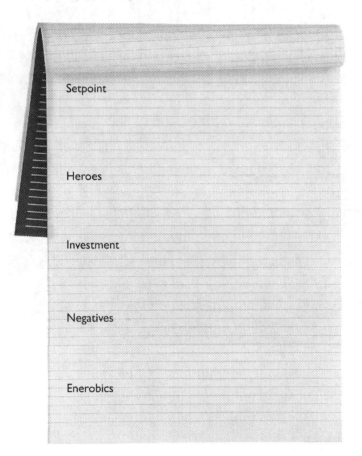

Setpoint

Heroes

Investment

Negatives

Enerobics

Plan Ahead

Sun	Mon	Tue	Wed	Thu	Fri	Sat
	1	2	3	4	5	6
7	8	9	10	11	12	13
14	15	16	17	18	19	20
21	22	23	24	25	26	27
28	29	30	31			

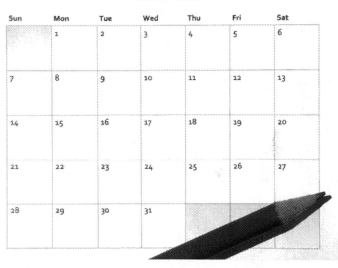

Sun	Mon	Tue	Wed	Thu	Fri	Sat
	1	2	3	4	5	6
7	8	9	10	11	12	13
14	15	16	17	18	19	20
21	22	23	24	25	26	27
28	29	30	31			

Things To Do

Plan Ahead
BUDGET WORKSHEET FOR STUDENTS

CATEGORY	MONTHLY BUDGET	SEMESTER BUDGET	SCHOOL YEAR BUDGET
SEMESTER INCOME:			
From Jobs			
From Parents			
From Student Loan			
From Scholarship			
From Financial Aid			
Miscellaneous Income			
INCOME SUBTOTAL			

SEMESTER EXPENSES:	Month 1	Month 2	Month 3	Month 4	Month 5	Month 6
Rent or Room & Board						
Utilities						
Telephone						
Groceries						
Car Payment/Transportation						
Insurance						
Gasoline/Oil						
Entertainment						
Eating Out/Vending						
Tuition/ Books						
School Fees						
Computer Expense						
Miscellaneous Expense						
EXPENSES SUBTOTAL						
NET INCOME (INCOME LESS EXPENSES)						

If an expense is incurred more or less often than monthly, convert it to a monthly amount when calculating the monthly budget amount. For instance, auto expense that is billed every six months would be converted to monthly by dividing the six month premium by six.

Contributors

Pat Blair Huntington, Ed.D., Author
Doctorate of Education, Master of Education
with Vocational Endorsement
Licensed Professional Counselor (Texas)
Texas Real Estate Broker
TEA Certifications in elementary classroom,
secondary administration, and career education
Professional experience as Risk Manager Safety
and Environmental Director
Multiple publications, trademarks, copyrights

Christine Cooper Oliphant, M.Ed.
Licensed Professional Counselor
Secondary School Counselor in Texas school districts
and private high schools.
Mother, Texas Rancher, Author

Katelyn Kitchens
Texas Tech University student
Reviewer, STAR POWER

Charles Weiner, CPA

Annie Willis
Texas Tech, Doctoral Student
Reviewer